Hey Alexa

Create me my own personal musical paradise

Who is the smartest person in the room? When asked, techy five-year-olds will tell you say that it is *Alexa*. There is no question that Alexa is always getting smarter—and more entertaining. With hundreds of thousands of supported commands, there are so many things to ask Alexa. Fun things. Sweet things. Helpful things. Factual things. Surprising things. So many things that it's tough to capture them all, but we think this book is a pretty good musical start. Try them out, just maybe not all at once.

In this book, you will learn how to use the most powerful musical orchestra for its size that has ever been created. It has every song imaginable by the original artists. And, you don't have to use vinyl discs or tapes or shiny CDs. It has no remote because you don't need one. If you can say *Alexa*, you can quickly have beautiful music playing anywhere in your home.

The Amazon Echo with its "Alexa Brain" listens to you, translating your voice into commands so it can play music. If that is not enough, it can turn the lights on, or order stuff from Amazon. ... Amazon calls the built-in brains of this device "*Alexa*," and she* is the thing that makes it work.

The Alexa technology used in the Amazon Echo devices from the Dot to the Generation 4 machines is quickly becoming the biggest non-secret in American and international life. Yet, when you get yours, you'll be compelled to tell everybody you know—thinking they don't know. Now that you've got it, you won't want to put this book down until you are ready to send your stereo console to the scrap heap or the Salvation Army.

It's a revolutionary change to home music. In fact it is like hauling your old stereo monster out with a huge hand truck and having a moving van replace it with a mini Ray Conniff, His Orchestra and Chorus, weighing in at just 10.55 ounces. Ray Conniff never sounded so good and his selections have improved over the years. You'll say that it is amazing .

by

B-R-I-A-N W. K-E-L-L-Y-

Title: Hey Alexa!
Subtitle: Teach me how to use your commands and playlists to make my home a musical paradise!
Copyright © December 2020, Brian W. Kelly;   Editor: Brian P. Kelly

All rights reserved: No part of this book may be reproduced or transmitted in any form, or by any means, electronic or mechanical, including photocopying, recording, scanning, faxing, or by any information storage and retrieval system, without permission from the publisher, LETS GO PUBLISH, in writing.

Disclaimer: Though judicious care was taken throughout the writing and the publication of this work that the information contained herein is accurate, there is no expressed or implied warranty that all information in this book is 100% correct. Therefore, neither LETS GO PUBLISH, nor the author accepts liability for any use of this work.

Trademarks: A number of products and names referenced in this book are trade names and trademarks of their respective companies.

Referenced Material: Standard Disclaimer: The information in this book has been obtained through personal and third-party observations, interviews, and copious research. Where unique information has been provided or extracted from other sources, those sources are acknowledged within the text of the book itself or in the References area in the front matter. Thus, there are no formal footnotes nor is there a bibliography section. Any picture that does not have a source was taken from various sites on the Internet with no credit attached. If resource owners would like credit in the next printing, please email publisher.

Published by: .... LETS GO PUBLISH!
Editor in Chief...Brian P. Kelly
Email: .... info@letsgopublish.com
Web site.. www.letsgopublish.com
Write to .... P.O. Box 621 Wilkes-Barre, PA 18703

Library of Congress Copyright Information Pending
Book Cover Design by **Brian W. Kelly**

Text Editor—Brian P. Kelly

ISBN Information: The International Standard Book Number (ISBN) is a unique machine-readable identification number, which marks any book unmistakably. The ISBN is the clear standard in the book industry. 159 countries and territories are officially ISBN members. The Official ISBN for this book is

978-1-951562-44-1

The price for this work is............. .... $9.95 **USD**

10   9   8   7   6   5   4   3   2   1

Release Date: .... December 2020

Dedication

I dedicate this book to my wonderful wife Patricia; our three wonderful
children Brian, Mike and Katie; and our friendly friends—Ben our always
very happy dog, who recently became an Angel, and
Buddy, our always cheerful Catholic cat
who now lives in Cat Heaven.

Thank You All!

Acknowledgments

I appreciate all the help that I have received in putting this book together as well as all of my other 258 other published books.

My printed acknowledgments had become so large that book readers "complained" about going through too many pages to get to page one of the text.

And, so to permit me more flexibility, I put my acknowledgment list online, and it continues to grow. Believe it or not, it once cost about a dollar more to print each book.

Thank you and God bless you all for your help.

Please check out www.letsgopublish.com to read the latest version of my heartfelt acknowledgments updated for this book. FYI, Wily Ky Eyely, my wonderful basketball playing "niece," loves this book and recommends it to all. She wants "Uncle Brian" to be our next US Senator but he's not running.

Click the bottom of the Main menu to see the big acknowledgments!

Thank you all!

Preface

Why did Brian Kelly write this book?

Brian Kelly loves music. This summer after seeing my daughter, Katie, and son, Brian Patrick commanding this hockey puck sized speaker around, I noticed what it can do. My son, Brian loves Madonna. To put it mildly, I have no such affinity. But, I love the Nitty Gritty Dirt Band and especially their hit Mr. Bojangles. So, when Brian came over to swim this summer and eventually he had to take a break, I tested my daughter's Alexa Dot to see if it would play songs for me.

When Brian came back from his break, he found Mr. Bojangles filling the back patio airwaves. I think he liked it. Then, I asked Alexa to play some Al Jolson, Roy Orbison, The Beatles, and the list goes on. Brian was swimming and he did not mind. I had no idea how to set up the Alexa for playing outdoors so once Brian left for the day, I was out of music 'til he came back and set it up again.

Eventually, I watched him set it up. Think of this. He unplugged the electrical cord from where my daughter kept Alexa and he plugged it in outside and placed it on a table. I waited to see which buttons he pushed and was very surprised that he pushed none. He immediately commanded "Alexa, play Madonna!" Alexa obediently played Madonna songs while I waited for his next break.

After Brian left that Sunday, I decided to try it myself the following Monday. It was a bright and sunny August day and I plugged Alexa in outside. I saw the lights flickering and when they stopped, I said, Alexa, play Mr. Bojangles. Alexa said playing Mr. Bojangles by the Nitty Gritty Band and then she played the song. It wasn't loud enough so I said, louder. When it finished, I said, "Again!" and Alexa played it again. I had mastered Alexa. It did not take much.

The second generation Echo Dot produced nice music but it was small and did not give the best sound. I asked my kids if they had other units. They told me yes, and I found them on the Internet. At the time, a taller device known as the Alexa 3rd Generation was available. At the same time, there was an Alexa II Plus that claimed to have third generation sound technology plus it has two other facilities. So, it is like an Echo 3 but it also has a built-in smarthome hub and a temperature sensor which the Echo III lacks. I paid the extra twenty bucks for the II Plus. I love it but I have not needed its extra facilities.

I was so thrilled with my own Echo II plus for about $79 that I wanted to share my experience with four family members. That's how much I love them. I went out to the Internet to see how much the Echo II Plus cost after I had mine for a month. I was surprised at all the differences. First of all the unit was discontinued but it was still available on specials.

The Echo 4 Gen had been announced along with new 4 Gen Dots that were shaped differently. I kept looking and I found the Echo II Plus at a closeout price of $59.00. The Echo 4 Gen was $99.00. I was very happy with the II Plus so I bought four of them.

Of the four units that arrived in less than two days, my sons Brian and Mike set their own up with no assistance almost immediately. My uncle Gerry still has not set his up. My sister Nancy invited my brother Joe and sister Mary and I and our spouses to her home for breakfast a while later.

While I was there I set up Nancy's Alexa. It was my first time. The toughest part was figuring out her iPhone password. Once we got that, we downloaded and set up the Alexa software on her phone. That was necessary to get the Alexa working. We followed the several instructions in the teeny Alexa manual and before we knew it, my sister's Alexa was pounding out great philharmonic music just like mine.

My mother's name was Irene and so on a lark, I said "Alexa, play Good Night Irene." Alexa announced that it would be sung by none other than Johnny Cash and that made the close of the day even more special. Alexa made our gathering much better than otherwise by providing the big band sound and selections galore. I think Alexa is one of the nicest things Amazon has ever given to the world.

Table of Contents

Chapter 1 Ya Gotta Love Alexa 17

Chapter 2 Where Did Alexa Come From? 21

Chapter 3 Amazon Echo Devices and Alexa 35

Chapter 4 Buying an Amazon Alexa Echo for Yourself 39

Chapter 5 Learning About Alexa by Loving Her to Pieces 57

Chapter 6 Alexa Music Commands, etc. 65

Other Books by Brian W. Kelly: (amazon.com, and Kindle) 75

About the Author

Brian W. Kelly retired as an Assistant Professor in the Business Information Technology (BIT) program at Marywood University, where he also served as the IBM i and Midrange Systems Technical Advisor to the IT Faculty. Kelly designed, developed, and taught many college and professional courses. He continues as a contributing technical editor to a number of IT industry magazines, including "The Four Hundred" and "Four Hundred Guru," published by IT Jungle.

Kelly is a former IBM Senior Systems Engineer and IBM Mid Atlantic Area Specialist. His specialty was designing applications for customers as well as implementing advanced IBM operating systems and software facilities on their machines.

He has an active information technology consultancy. He is the author of 258 books and numerous technical articles. Kelly has been a frequent speaker at COMMON, IBM conferences, and other technical conferences.

Brian was a candidate for US Congress from Pennsylvania in 2010 and Mayor from his home town in 2015. Other than a tradition of winning elections, Brian brings a lot of experience to his writing endeavors.

Chapter 1 Ya Gotta Love Alexa

For most of this past summer (2020) and into the fall, I would say: "Hey Alexa, play Mr. Bojangles!" Then, Alexa dutifully would wake up and speak:

"Mr. Bojangles, remastered by the Nitty Gritty Dirt Band on Amazon Music." The next sounds would come from the song:

> *I knew a man Bojangles and he danced for you*
> *In worn out shoes*
> *Silver hair, a ragged shirt and baggy pants*
> *The old soft shoe*

This great song is one of my all-time favorites. When I was just over 21-years of age, I jointly owned a bar in Parsons, PA, just outside of Wilkes-Barre with my recently RIP buddy George Mohanco. We liked the theme of the Bojangles song so much that we named our new bar "Mr. Bojangles." Such a great experience and the song brings back all those great memories. The Alexa II sound makes it sound like Bojangles is tapdancing to a philharmonic.

There was no Alexa back in the 1970's. But, the corner Wurlitzer, A hot coin-operated jukebox, served as the partially automated music-playing machine. It was a coin-activated v voice-activated unit.

The coin woke up the Juke Box and played our patron's selection from self-contained media. Our jukebox had buttons, with letters and numbers on them, which, when one of each group were entered after each other, it selected a specific record. In our case, the most played song was Mr. Bojangles. Today the most played voice activated song on my Echo II Plus is Mr. Bojangles. Sounded great then. Sounds even better today.

I first met Alexa at the family Christmas gathering at my nephew Scott's home in Harrisburg in 2016. My sister-in-law Sue brought an Echo Dot as her donated prize for a Dirty Bingo game. She said she had gotten a great deal with the unit costing her about $20.00. Some of the family thought she paid more, which violated the Dirty Bingo rules. But that's Sue—generous to a fault.

I think my brother-in-law Marty got final possession of the Echo Dot at the end of the Dirty Bingo game. I never saw him use it but I am sure he loves it like I love mine. Nobody knew what the Amazon Echo Dot was at first but everybody seemed interested.

In short while the Internet had explained all. I recall that no member of our high tech family made Alexa wake up and by the end of the night, to me and others, it was still a mystery. But, we had seen it and felt it. .

Some had seen things like the Dot before. I had no idea what it was. Worse than that; I did not even care. Nephew Scott had some fine libations to which I was preoccupied. I am not even sure I was in the Dirty Bingo game. I had a nice stool in the open kitchen. But I do recall seeing this thing that looked like an attractive grey hockey-puck. It was Amazon's first real Echo device known as the Dot.

A year or so later, ahem, as usual, I reached deep into my wallet for my wife's Christmas present. As part of a bundle for her iRobot, was tan Amazon Echo Dot. I still did not understand what it was all about. My brother Joe set it all up for my wife so that it would respond to the name Brian W. I was still oblivious.

It was not until this summer that I became interested again in Alexa. Alexa, start the next chapter. Oh, never mind kiddo, I'll do that.

Chapter 2 Where Did Alexa Come From?

Before you consider buying this great product, I must remind you that Amazon Echo is one of the most strategically planned products ever from Amazon and it is still in its infancy. Echo is the hardware and Alexa is the controlling brain. Amazon boasts of over 5000 developers and engineers working on this product to make it better, better, better.. ah! I am happy just using its voice recognition and musical connections and right now, at least, my personal Echo-lust goes no further.

The Amazon Echo family at a point in *me*

It turns out the idea of the echo had been kicked around in the Amazon Labs from 2011 when it was viewed by the company as one of the promises upon which to bet for the future. The company's founder Jeff Bezos was very interested in the project and so it was one of those things that had little problem receiving organizational funding and support. The Amazon company was not about to fail its boss.

The original goals for the Echo was for it to become "an intelligent, voice-controlled household appliance that could play music, read the news aloud and order groceries — all by simply letting users talk to it from anywhere in the house." Amazingly from where I stand, Amazon achieved its goal and now it is on to continual improvements as in 1.2, 2.0, 2.1, 3.0 etc. just like DOS and Windows from the 1980's. A higher version or generation number always means a better mousetrap.

Alexa "the voice enabler," aka, the digital assistant, was first launched on the Amazon Echo in November 2014. The Echo at the time was a small piece of hardware shaped like a hockey puck. It was the Echo Dot. Alexa came with it. The combination was initially only available to invited Amazon Prime members. General release for the Echo and Alexa was June 2015

Echo is a small machine in a class of devices and voices known as digital assistants. Before digital assistants could ever be invented, however, PC-like machines and chips had to be able to understand the human voice. This phenomenon is known as *voice recognition*. The capability that gives a machine the ability to speak is called *voice synthesis*. Recognition is much more difficult than synthesis. Alexa, the "brain" of the Amazon Echo line of machines performs both voice recognition and voice synthesis.

IBM and other technology research firms were leaders in the difficult task of voice recognition. In August 1981, IBM invented The Personal Computer (PC) and from there the digital revolution using the word "personal" began. The primary device used to "talk" to PCs in the 1980's was the keyboard and then the mouse and then an array of other input devices.

Human speech was very difficult for computers to learn to understand and so it eluded researchers in the 1980s but incremental gains and inventions continued to be made. In the 1990s digitalspeech recognition technology was perfected and it became a feature of the personal computer.

IBM, Philips, and Lemout & Hauspie in the research days were fighting for speech recognition customers. A few years later, IBM launched the first smartphone known as IBM Simon in 1994. This laid the foundation for smart virtual digital assistants as we know them today.

According to industry analysts twenty years ago, speech recognition technology was one of top technology trends to watch for the next two to five years. "Speech recognition will drive innovation in user interfaces over the next decade. "The Philips-IBM strategic relationship accelerated market growth and made it easier to launch truly international products," according to William Meisel, President, TMA Associates, a speech industry consulting firm." The Echo with Alexa and all the other personal digital assistants of today are the beneficiaries of all this advanced research. Alexa, "say it is so."

The experts see digital assistants as being the next revolution in computing. We all believe it because we have begun to see it happen. iPhones have Siri; Google has its Assistant, Microsoft has Cortana, and of course Alexa is all Amazon's.

These technologies can get you results with nothing but a voice command.

Alexa, has clearly dominated the digital assistant market space in the past few years. I even know about it. It has quickly become a household name. Amazon established an early foothold in the war for digital assistant supremacy, but for those who don't use Alexa or one of its competitors, there's still the question of what exactly they are. When we answer the question of what is Alexa, we have answered the question of what is a digital assistant.

What is Alexa?

Ask that question of your web browser and here is what you will get:

The Amazon Echo listens to you, translating your voice into commands so it can play music, turn the lights on, or order stuff from Amazon. ... Amazon calls the built-in brains of this device "Alexa," and she* is the thing that makes it work.

For this book, we concentrate on describing Alexa and the Echo product and of course, we show the user how to make the most of the product's music facilities. But, like above, we also give a few revealing tid-bits of other capabilities of these fascinating Amazon devices.

With Alexa having turned six-years old in 2020, the Kindergarten-aged "platform" with Alexa in control is destined to teach the rest of the tech world and more than likely the rest of the education industry. Those who know me or who have looked me up, may know that just last week, before I began this book, I published my 258th book.

For each paperback book that I write, I create a corresponding e-book, or as Amazon calls it a Kindle book. See below. A picture is worth a thousand words. Kindle can be an Alexa device. Below, see a Kindle Ad.

FYI, you can also read my kindle books or anybody else's online without the kindle reader hardware shown above. You don't even need Alexa. You can use the Kindle cloud reader which is a web app developed by Amazon for reading with any web browser (Google Chrome, Internet Explorer, Safari and Firefox). It enables you to read Kindle books without downloading any app.

Alexa is clearly ubiquitous. Many homes have more than one. Some homes have lots more than one. Some have an Amazon Alexa device in every room in their house and two or three in certain rooms. If you want to keep in touch with all of your Amazon devices, it is getting easier and easier with Alexa. You can integrate Echo's with Amazon's Fire TV devices, the Kindle e-readers discussed above, and, of course, with other Amazon's digital assistant, Alexa.

I am writing this book in November 2020. It was just six years ago, on Nov. 6, 2014 that Amazon announced the original Echo speaker. At that time, the unit cost $199 (or $99 for Amazon Prime members). This was the "launch" price.

We already discussed how this "smart speaker" was originally available by invitation only, for the first few months. The test versions were out for over a year, when it seemed that all at once, regular consumers were enabled to buy an Echo.

My sister-in-law Sue, swears she got an Echo Dot with Alexa for $19.99 at least three years ago in time for Dirty Bingo. Maybe! Nonetheless, the public bought them up like candy bars as soon as they became available.

The Dot is a price-performer for sure. In 2019 Amazon said it had sold more than 100 million Alexa-compatible devices. I would expect that number to be approaching 1 billion today. That's how ubiquitous Alexa has become. Alexa devices fit into a new category which doesn't come along in consumer electronics very often.

Amazon had a lot to overcome to be successful with Alexa. The major obstacle was that Amazon per se, was not known as a hardware company. The company achieved success as a mass distributor of products made by others. Its prior Fire

Phone effort was a complete flop and so failure was another option that Amazon's new venture had to overcome.

Since the Fire phone and the Echo speaker were developed at about the same time by "Lab126," it was clear Amazon was willing to use its other vast resources to take risks to see which innovations would connect with customers. Alexa and the Echo units made it big-time. There is no need for second guessing this tremendous success.

One of the ways Amazon was able to speed things to market with less potential failures was to use standard available parts when possible rather than inventing it all internally, Amazon decided to make it easy for other developers to plug their apps into Alexa's code, and to plug Alexa's code into all kinds of third party devices. That is why the Echo with Alexa was able to catch on so quickly. Amazon's Alexa is an open platform, being able to connect means it is "open."

Other developers have been out in the marketplace busy making their units work with Alexa. They figure when Alexa is successful—now—they will get some of that success. Each time a developer builds another capability, Amazon considers it another Alexa "skill." Today, there are well over 100,000 skills, besides music, my favorite.

The skills allow Alexa users to play word games, hear jokes, access their calendars, translate from one language to another, and more. And on the hardware side, Amazon itself has rolled out a massive array of Alexa-compatible devices—everything from televisions and thermostats to headphones, microwave ovens, and other clever implementations of voice-enabled technology.

Partnership with outside developers have brought the Alexa "brain" and sound to popular products. Perhaps you have seen such brands as Fitbit smartwatches and Sonos high-end speakers. If not, watch out!

Alexa can now come with your new GM vehicle and can even be retrofitted into older models. It can do everything in your car that you would do with it at home. Drivers can control the lights or climate and even add items to their Amazon shopping cart. You know now! Therefore, don't be shy about ordering toilet paper on the go for the go. Since fingers are not required, maybe the Charmin Bears can also make a nice TP order so they can stay clean.

Amazon plans to extend its openness even further. The executives are saying that they are willing to share their platform with other digital assistants. "The whole pie is getting bigger as customers are embracing this technology," Tom Taylor, who heads the Alexa effort, boasted to Fortune. "As we look at the future of these voice assistants, we don't think that you just have one any more than you would just have one friend." At $18 bucks a piece for a Dot 3 Gen on Black Friday 2020, Amazon put its money where its Alexa mouth is.

Of course if you have no Echo today, one is a good enough start. Alexa can be controlling your music within ten minutes out of the box and the music will melt your heart.

Over time, Alexa has also grown more complex and more capable. Smart home control wasn't even foreseen as a possible use case by Amazon engineers initially. Now, besides music, my favorite and my reason for writing this book, it has become one of the most popular functions.

Drivers buzzing by cities now see more light action than ever with users controlling household lights by voice and inside, they control the thermostats, and many other items. It is easy but let's get you listening to your favorite tunes first.

I have a young uncle Gerry who has had his $59.00 Alexa II Plus for almost two months now and he has not taken it out of the box yet. He knows like every other new Alexa user, to begin his installation and set-up, he needs to download the Alexa App to his cell phone. He is stuck right there. He confessed to one of my other buddies, Denny Bucko that he does not want to be spied on by Amazon. Denny does not think Gerry will ever get his Alexa going because he is afraid of "Big Amazon." We'll see!

There was a time when there was a need for privacy concerns and perhaps there still is a little. It was widely reported that a Geekwire reviewer highlighted that Alexa users did not completely understand that their computers (Echo) had given access to their data and recordings that had been collected and shared—even just within Amazon.

After a few minor incidents, like police officers seeking Alexa recordings, in one case to investigate a murder, the privacy issue had to be addressed by Amazon this year.

Reporters discovered that there were thousands of people who worked for Amazon, listening to a small portion of Alexa customer recordings for good reason—in order to improve the system's voice recognition and other features.

Some critics charged that Amazon hadn't been clear that its employees could listen to customer recordings.

The Amazon Executive in charge said "We thought we were telling customers clearly and we thought it was a pretty known industry thing." Humans had been reviewing users' dictation recordings and map requests and other data collected by their devices.

Regular people were in the loop on all these things. The company thought it had been communicating its concerns and solutions well enough. But, with the recent blowback, even Amazon learned it had not done enough to alleviate the public fears. That was yesterday and yesterday's gone.

As a result of the findings, Amazon addressed the issues with vigor. The company improved its policies on disclosure and customer control. For example, users can now opt out completely of having their recordings reviewed by other humans.

Users can also review and delete their recordings. One can certainly give Amazon credit for making it much better than when nobody saw collecting data as a problem. Maybe my buddy Gerry will start listening to music one day soon.

By the way, my uncle, Gerry Rodski plays often with a great local group known as The Music Room from NEPA. He is a pro and has a massive guitar selection. If Amazon can convince Uncle Gerry they are safe, he is a reasonable man and will surely support their efforts. Come on Ger!

If Alexa was not so unique and so powerful a device, it would not be so pervasive. As we have been discussing, Alexa, of course, is Amazon's very capable artificially intelligent assistant. It first appeared in the Echo "smart" speaker. She has this always-listening microphone array, and she has the means to respond to your voice commands and execute your requests.

If you do not ask nicely, in other words if you are rude, sarcastic or vulgar, Alexa is trained to give you the short shrift. Ask nicely and you can stream something to your stereo; watch something on TV, check the news, traffic, and weather reports, order a pizza, and, not surprisingly, you can buy stuff from Amazon.

With 3,000 recognizable commands at last count, and with the count growing every day, the "voice lady" is probably about 2,995 words more conversant than your neighbor's dog. After all, the neighbor's dog never seems to be listening to reason. Alexa listens to everything.

Independent experts believe that soon, everything will have an Alexa (or Siri, Cortana, or Google Assistant) patiently listening as an electronic servant. And admittedly, having a voice assistant hovering ubiquitously as a supplicant minion, it may create out of our once capable bodies, the need for a "Graham," the creepy crash guy shown on the next page. Remember him?

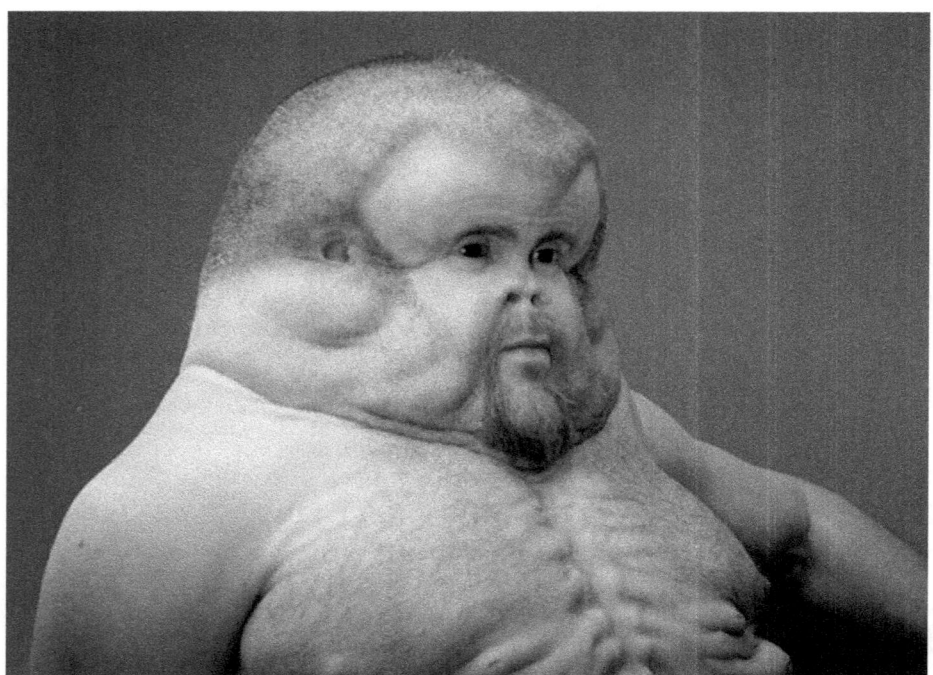

Graham – not a real person but an amalgam of what not using your body parts will bring.

One of my worst fears is that using just voice commands rather than arms and legs and hands and feet, after a while, thanks to Alexa, we might all evolve to look something like Graham—above. Whatever we need, we'll just ask, and Alexa will provide.

"Our heads will grow big and neckless because we'll never need to take our eyes off our big screens. Our bellies will grow fat because we'll never need to leave our La-Z-Boys. Our arms will be skinny because of lack of use and mostly wither away because we won't even have to pick up the remote.

Am I telling the truth? Well, let's try it with music. Suppose you wanted to hear "I Should Have Known Better" In the old days, you had to walk over to your record shelf, find your Beatles Albums, then, A Hard Days Night, then play it on the stereo, and move the needle to the second song on side A.

Now, in the electronics age, you just press a few buttons on your browser or phone. With Alexa and her friends, it is even easier. You won't even need to move your fingers. No phone or keyboard necessary either. Just sit there! Ask Alexa. She will be happy to help you, even if your name is not yet Graham.

Chapter 3 Amazon Echo Devices and Alexa

Everybody knows who and what Amazon is all about. For many, Amazon had represented their first online book purchase and now almost anything else in the online purchasing category. The company surely seems to know what it is doing.

Amazon became the most valuable public company in the world after passing Microsoft. Then, Apple passed Amazon. Amazon is now the No. 2 American company by market cap (total value of shares).

It is quickly approaching the $2 trillion benchmark. The Company has many achievements. Making the Echo and inventing Alexa are only part of their story. You can read lots about Amazon if you like. For our purposes, know that they can afford to make as many Echos with Alexa as the people want each year. The Amazon product will be smarter and provide more for the purchaser's dollar as time rolls by.

The picture on the next page is as Lewis and Clark would say is of a pioneer—an Amazon pioneer—the Echo 2. I have had one at home for two years. It came with my wife's iRobot. As great a product as the Echo Dot 2 is, Amazon is not alone in the race of high tech voice-enabled devices. Amazon may not be the only game in town anymore but the company is clearly #1 in the race.

The Amazon Echo Dot 2

Alexa as we have discussed briefly is the voice assistant on Amazon devices, equivalent to Apple's Siri, Microsoft's Cortana, and Google's Google Assistant. Siri is second in popularity to Alexa and is available across most of Apple's devices, including iPhone, iPad, Mac, Apple Watch, Apple TV, and the HomePod.

Amazon has more competitors every day but the Echo line is more than holding its own. Some other biggies include

Google's Assistant and its NEST, Samsung's Bixby, Apple's Homepod, and Microsoft's Cortana. They are all in the same market territory with their own special units. Amazon is the company bringing in over 60% of the bacon.

This book focuses on the music facilities and commands in Amazon's Echo series with Alexa. However, it's you, who have to decide which Echo hardware unit is best to serve as your personal "smart speaker" with artificial intelligence abilities. Alexa, the cute indescribable *Echo Brain* would be happy to host any of your Amazon devices. Alexa can also control home units through smartplugs and smart thermostats etc.

This book is mostly about using your Echo for music. Once you master music, the entire world of Alexa is your oyster. There are other more sophisticated Amazon devices that you can use as your intelligent speakers but once we show you how to master the Echo, if you choose to up your device ante, it will all come easier.

We talk about music in this book but there is a whole other world available for Alexa-enabled products. Remember unknowingly Brian W (my name and the iRobot's name) became Alexa's name to operate my wife's iRobot. My brother set it up that way as a joke. Now, I know enough to set Alexa up myself.

Which brand will you say fulfils your needs the best? I made up my mind reading the available research and of course the great ads for the various units on the Internet. After checking out many smart speakers and doing light research about each of the main players in this space, my opinion is that Alexa as an idea and a realization is ahead of all its competitors. The Echo is all you need to get going. It's what you find in all of your friend's home's today.

Amazon Echo in all its generations is quite a device. It is a hybrid speaker that not only broadcasts sound, it understands voices. Its voice recognition will answer your questions and can manage a number of particular tasks. We'll discuss how to set it up soon and then we'll show you how to bring the Alexa philharmonic music sounds into any room of your home.

In the next chapter we lightly discuss the Echo models that Amazon provides. Just about all of the models, even those that are not the most current are still available from various sources. The Internet is the best place to do your Alexa shopping.

Chapter 4 Buying an Amazon Alexa Echo for Yourself

Amazon Echo (4Th Gen) with Premium Sound, Smart Home Hub, and Alexa- Charcoal

Item #3209483 Model #B07XKF5RM3

More than likely, you bought this book to help you understand all of the musical treats that would come your way with your very own Alexa. You may not have your Alexa yet, or like Uncle Gerry it is still in its box. For those of you in the former category this chapter will tell you where

Alexa Echo came from and what models are out there and available for you to bring home as your own.

The Amazon Echo itself was first dreamed up in 2011 and soon, about ten years ago it blossomed into a project known internally as "Project D."

Where there is a "D", most often there is an "A." FYI, Project A was the development of *Kindle* and Project B was the *Fire Phone*. The Echo came about from the work on Project C though whatever Project C was intended to be, it was never completed. The Echo was a major fruit of the project.

Amazon's Echo thus came from the remains of a defunct project. It was supposed to be named the Amazon *Flash*. But the Flash never saw the light of day.

Amazon's Lab 126 in Amazon was responsible for the work with the project. Let's take a side trail for a bit here to discuss one of the decisions about the Echo project. If you have not heard of such a term yet as a *"wake word."* This next paragraph will "wake you up" to the word.

There is this notion called the "wake word," which as they say is the word that makes a device responsive to voice commands. It is a word that wakes up the device so that it listens to commands. The default wake word for the Echo is now *Alexa*. Say Alexa and you'll know what I mean.

When you want the unit to do something such as play your favorite music, you say the wake word, Alexa, and the Alexa then begins to listen to your commands to her. Well, it was not always so easy when there was a dispute over the wake word in the Amazon Lab.

You see, there were those who wanted the wake word to be Amazon. Amazon's Development Lab 126 did not like the word Amazon as a wake word. This is important because Lab126 is an important division in the company that performs the research and development and then creates the computer hardware for the Echo device.

"*Amazon*" was perceived by this group to be a too commonly used word, and they were concerned that their device would react and wake up too often--when it was not intended to. For example, the speakers would wake upon hearing Amazon ads on television and begin buying random stuff from the Internet. This seems like it would help business but surely not for long.

The boss, Jeff Bezos, who is the founder and CEO of Amazon, made the decision in favor of the Lab 126 engineers. The company then changed the name of the hardware to the Amazon Echo and the wake-up word to "Alexa". Now you know the rest of the story and you can win at your next trivia game.

Here are some additional trivia secrets for your next victory party. Despite Alexa being the default, the Echo now permits the user to change the wake word. You can't change Alexa's name as imprinted on your Amazon speaker, but you can change your speaker's "wake word" to one of several other available terms.

As noted, the Amazon speakers are set to listen for the name "Alexa" as its default "wake word, but you can change it to either "Amazon," "Echo," or "computer." Neat, right? The process is easy but many users get their smart phone out to set a new "wake word." It can be done remotely via the app, or directly through your device speaker.

Some more trivia is that The Amazon Echo was originally intended only to become a smart speaker. It was not originally supposed to be a smart home hub, as it is now. That did not happen until the first echo hit the market.

As *Alexa*, the brain, aka, the artificial intelligence (A.I.) that powers the Amazon Echo, kept improving, the unit became more of a controlling center for smart home appliances.

Before the public appeared reluctant to buy smart home appliances, computer developers could not wait to make their devices compatible with Alexa. In fact, the chief Amazon developer who was also the evangelist for Echo and Alexa, Dave Isbitski, received calls from smart home manufacturers to discuss connecting their devices, after the initial release of the Amazon Echo.

The only problem as noted was that people were not buying them because in the early days of smart homes, they were often disappointing. The current vision for the Echo has been enhanced for it to be more of the controlling hub of a smart home. Everything keeps improving.

Despite not initially meeting its intended first market, the 1st Generation Amazon Echo was released in March 2014 for Amazon Prime. More trivia is that the voice of Alexa was inspired by the systems in both the television series Star Trek: The Original Series and Star Trek: The Next Generation.

In March 2016 Amazon released a byproduct of the Amazon Echo, which brought the device into what we recognize today as the Amazon Echo Dot. This unit is the hockey puck sized version of the original Amazon Echo with the same capabilities. It was put together to be used in smaller rooms such as bedrooms and it can be paired with an external speaker for sound amplification.

Eight months later in November 2016 version 2.0 was released as the second generation of the Echo Dot. It had a much lower price with highly tuned voice recognition and attractive new colors new colors.

This is not a tech book so we are not providing much more than the origin of the product and its basic specifications and capabilities so you have a decent perspective. There is a lot to know because every day Amazon has 5000 or more developers working on improvements to the Echo device

The specifications of the current models and the price ranges that regular people pay today come right from Amazon on the Internet. We than Amazon for telling us all we need to know. The Echo product begins on the following page. Pictures are stock pictures from Amazon used to market their products. If you think you have seen these products in Amazon ads it is because more than likely you have. Our arrangement makes the product line easier to understand. Here they are:

All-new Echo Dot (4th Gen) | Smart speaker with Alexa | Charcoal (4 colors)

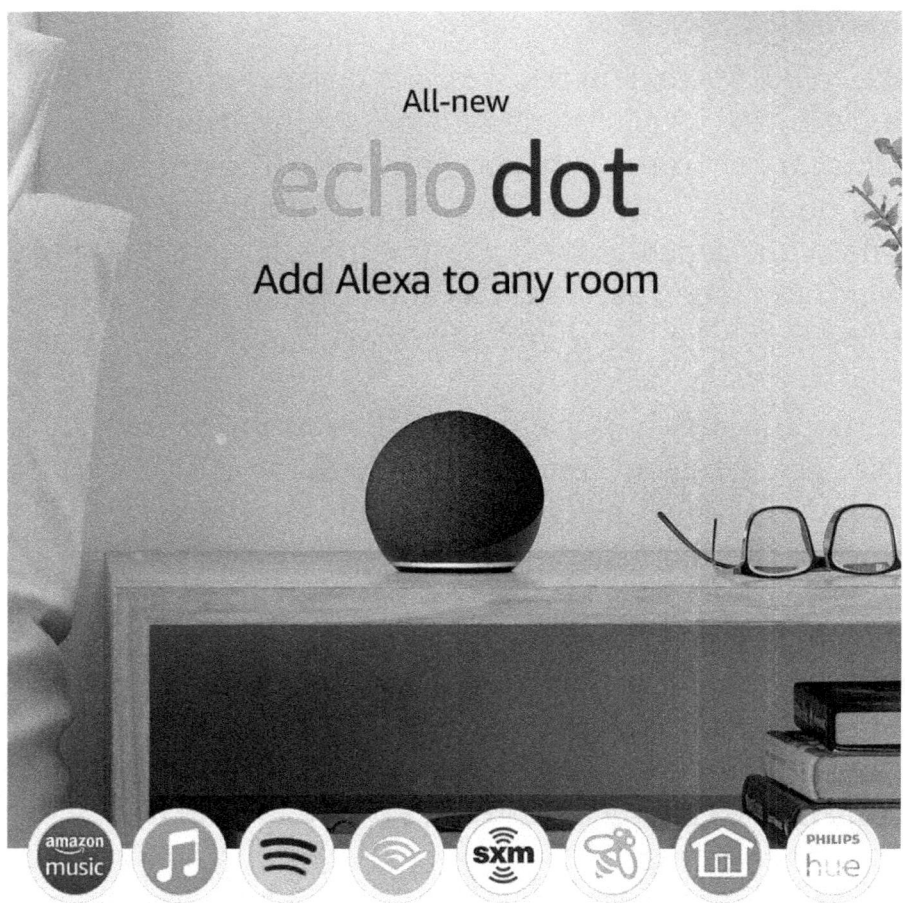

Meet the all-new Echo Dot - Our most popular smart speaker with Alexa. The sleek, compact design delivers crisp vocals and balanced bass for full sound.
Voice control your entertainment - Stream songs from Amazon Music, Apple Music, Spotify, SiriusXM, and others. Play music, audiobooks, and podcasts throughout your home with multi-room music.

Ready to help - Ask Alexa to tell a joke, play music, answer questions, play the news, check the weather, set alarms, and more.

Control your smart home - Use your voice to turn on lights, adjust thermostats, and lock doors with compatible devices.

Connect with others - Call almost anyone hands-free.

Instantly drop in on other rooms or announce to the whole house that dinner's ready.

Designed to protect your privacy - Built with multiple layers of privacy protections and controls, including a microphone off button that electronically disconnects the microphones.

Echo Dot (3rd Gen) - Smart speaker with Alexa – Charcoal (4 colors)

Meet Echo Dot - Our most popular smart speaker with a fabric design. It is our most compact smart speaker that fits perfectly into small spaces.

Improved speaker quality - Better speaker quality than Echo Dot Gen 2 for richer and louder sound. Pair with a second Echo Dot for stereo sound.

Voice control your music - Stream songs from Amazon Music, Apple Music, Spotify, Sirius XM, and others.

Ready to help - Ask Alexa to play music, answer questions, read the news, check the weather, set alarms, control compatible smart home devices, and more.

Voice control your smart home - Turn on lights, adjust thermostats, lock doors, and more with compatible connected devices. Create routines to start and end your day.

Connect with others - Call almost anyone hands-free. Instantly drop in on other rooms in your home or make an announcement to every room with a compatible Echo device.

Alexa has skills - With tens of thousands of skills and counting, Alexa is always getting smarter and adding new skills like tracking fitness, playing games, and more.

Designed to protect your privacy - Built with multiple layers of privacy protections and controls, including a microphone off button that electronically disconnects the microphones.

The second generation of the Amazon Echo was released in October 2017. This update offered better voice recognition and a fabric covering exterior. Since this many other variants of the Amazon Echo have been released.

In May 2017 Amazon released the now-discontinued Amazon Tap, a portable, slightly smaller version of the Amazon Echo. Although the two products are similar the

Tap is battery powered, portable, and requires the touch of a button in order to enable voice commands.

In April 2017 the Amazon Echo Look was released to invitees only, as an Amazon Echo with a built in camera. It was designed as a speaker, that is also handy with artificial intelligence that has smart algorithms to help you pick out outfits. It was released to the general public in August 2018.

In June 2018 the Amazon Echo Show was released to the public as a device with a 7-inch screen used for streaming media, making video calls, and the use of Alexa. The second generation of the device was made available in November 2018 and features a 10-inch screen with improved speakers.

All-new Echo (4th Gen) | With premium sound, smart home hub, and Alexa | Charcoal (4 colors)

New look, new sound - Echo delivers clear highs, dynamic mids, and deep bass for rich, detailed sound that automatically adapts to any room.

Amazon Echo (4th Gen)

Voice control your entertainment - Stream songs from Amazon Music, Apple Music, Spotify, SiriusXM, and more. Plus listen to radio stations, podcasts, and Audible audiobooks.

Ready to help - Ask Alexa to play music, answer questions, play the news, check the weather, set alarms, control compatible smart home devices, and more.

Smart home made simple - With the built-in hub, easily set up compatible Zigbee devices or Ring Smart Lighting products (coming soon) to voice control lights, locks, and sensors.

Fill your home with sound - With multi-room music, play synchronized music across Echo devices in different rooms. Or pair your Echo with compatible Fire TV devices to feel scenes come to life with home theater audio.

Connect with others - Call almost anyone hands-free. Instantly drop in on other rooms or announce to the whole house that dinner's ready.

Designed to protect your privacy - Built with multiple layers of privacy protections and controls, including a microphone off button that electronically disconnects the microphones.

Echo (3rd Gen)- Smart speaker with Alexa- Charcoal. This device is **Currently** unavailable. Amazon has not suggested when or if this item will be back in stock.

Meet Echo - Echo (3rd Gen) has new premium speakers powered by Dolby to play 360° audio with crisp vocals and dynamic bass response.

Enjoy premium sound - Personalize your listening experience by adjusting the equalizer settings. Pair with a second Echo (3rd Gen) or Echo Plus (2nd Gen) for stereo sound and add more bass with an Echo Sub.

Voice control your music - Ask Alexa for a song, artist, or genre from Amazon Music, Apple Music, Spotify, Pandora, SiriusXM, and more. With multi-room music, play music on compatible Echo devices in different rooms.

Echo (3rd Gen)- Smart speaker with Alexa

Voice control your smart home - Turn on lights, adjust thermostats, lock doors, and more with compatible connected devices.

Keep your family in sync - Use your Alexa devices like an intercom and talk to any room in the house with Drop In and Announcements.

Alexa has skills - With tens of thousands of skills and counting, Alexa is always getting smarter and adding new skills like tracking fitness, playing games, and more.

Designed to protect your privacy - Built with multiple layers of privacy controls, including a microphone off button that electronically disconnects the mics.

Echo Plus (2nd Gen) - Premium sound with built-in smart home hub - Heather Gray
Brand: Amazon 4.7 out of 5 stars   86,369 ratings 1000+ answered questions
Currently unavailable. Amazon does not know when or if this item will be back in stock.

I bought four of these Echo II Plus devices on October 7 from Amazon for $59.00. They work great.
There is no difference between these four and the new one I bought for $74.99.

Certified Refurbished Echo Plus (2nd Gen) - Premium sound with built-in smart home hub - Dark Charcoal Sold by: Amazon.com Services LLC.

I was so impressed with my own Alex that I received on September 4, 2020, that a month later I bought for for close family members. They were thrilled -especially Uncle Gerry though he has not asked to have his set up yet....soon?.

Echo Plus (2nd Gen) - Premium sound with built-in smart home hub - Charcoal
Sold by: Amazon.com Services LLC   Return eligibility $74.99   Condition: New

Meet the Echo Plus - Same great sound as our Echo (3rd Gen) with a built-in Zigbee hub to easily setup and control your compatible smart home devices.

Enjoy premium sound - Personalize your listening experience by adjusting the equalizer settings. Or pair with a second Echo Plus (2nd Gen) or Echo (3rd Gen) for stereo sound and add more bass with an Echo Sub.

Voice control your music - Ask Alexa for a song, artist, or genre from Amazon Music, Apple Music, Spotify, Pandora, SiriusXM, and more.

With multi-room music, play music on compatible Echo devices in different rooms.

Voice control your smart home - Turn on lights, adjust thermostats, lock doors, and more with compatible connected devices. Create routines to start and end your day.

Keep your family in sync - Use your Alexa devices like an intercom and talk to any room in the house with Drop In and Announcements.

Alexa has skills - With tens of thousands of skills and counting, Alexa is always getting smarter and adding new skills like tracking fitness, playing games, and more.

Designed to protect your privacy - Built with multiple layers of privacy controls, including a microphone off button that electronically disconnects the mics.

What are the 4 buttons on Alexa?

The top of the echo dot has four buttons, four microphones and an LED ring. The + and – buttons control the volume, the white circle activates Alexa and the circle with a line through it enables or disables the microphones. Jul 21, 2019

The difference is that the new model has its speaker forward-firing, whereas the old Echo Dot (3rd Generation) has its speaker firing upwards.

The main difference is that the new Dot (4th Generation) is clearer and louder than the previous model.   Oct 29, 2020

Which Alexa is best?

From November 20, 2020

Our pick. Amazon Echo (3rd Gen) The best basic Alexa speaker. ...

Budget pick. Amazon Echo Dot. A good Alexa speaker if sound quality isn't important. ...

Upgrade pick. Sonos One. The best Alexa speaker for whole-house music. ...

Also great. Ultimate Ears Megablast. The best Alexa speaker for backyards. ...

Also great. Marshall Stanmore II Voice.

Is Alexa worth buying?

Take it from me, a new user from early September, 2020. Yes, Alexa is worth buying, and it comes down to the simple fact that it can make your life easier and more fun.

Here Amazon is, a few years into the product and there are thousands of "Alexa Skills" and devices that work with Alexa that can do everything from play music to control your smart thermostat and many other things. Check the Internet and there are more available every day. Don't forget about the 5000 developers working for Amazon thinking every minute of the day what they can do to please you.

Last question til next chapter: Is Alexa dangerous?

No, But! You're probably thinking, "Does it really matter where I put it as long as I can speak to Alexa from most areas in my house?" Our answer is yes. Placing your Alexa device in certain areas of your house could risk your privacy, security or even damage your Echo.

Here is a note from September 5, 2020

Keep your Amazon Echo in a safe place.
Sarah Tew/CNET
Your Amazon Echo is there to help when it comes to setting up your preferred music streaming service and setting

reminders. However, it doesn't tell you the best and safest areas in your house to place the smart speaker.

Are you now thinking, "Does it really matter where I put it as long as I can speak to Alexa from most areas in my house?" Amazon's answer is yes.

Placing your Alexa device in certain areas of your house could risk your privacy, security or even damage your Echo.

For example, did you know intruders can access your smart speaker from outside if it's placed too close to a window?

We're here to tell you where you shouldn't place your Echo speaker and the best spots for it. Check the Internet or ask your Alexa for more information.

Two more things. Take a peek at the First Echo model

Now, look at the deal that exists today as I finish this chapter. Amazon Echo Dot is available for Black Friday. I sent the ad out to my buddies and they thanked me.

Chapter 5 Learning About Alexa by Loving Her to Pieces

My buddy Mike Grant loves Alexa. He also loves Music. Mike and I were buddies back in St. Therese's Little League and we played baseball on the Meyers High School Baseball team. When we were not in our usual positions at practice, he and I and a few other Mohawks would group together in the outfield either shagging flies or "watching" batting practice waiting for that few and far between lonely baseball to fly our way. Then came the music but Alexa was 55 years away.

The Beatles had just become popular and the British Invasion was in full progress. In the outfield we did our best harmony with the Beatles "All My Loving," our fava. We were pretty good but not as good as Alexa. Then in Gym class while changing for a shower unsupervised, with just a wall separating the boys from the girls locker rooms, Mike and I and others would bellow out the Dave Clark Five's "Glad All Over."

At the exact right time, when we sang, "Baby, I'm" [INSERT] "Glad All Over!", at the insert point, we would strategically pound as hard as we could on the boy's lockers (conscious that the girls would hear us). We all agreed that we sounded even better than the original song—the symbols part at least.

Today, the two of us still like those tunes and we get to hear them without each others' help by saying Alaxa, play "All My Lovin or we can say, Alexa, play "Glad all over." It's not like being in the boy's locker room but it is the next best thing.

Michael Grant and I have maintained our friendship over the years I am pleased to say. Though we are not aligned politically we more than get along. He and his wife Mo and my wife Pat and I in non-COVID years have enjoyed summer dances at the Irem Country Club with Joe Nardone and the All-Stars dancing to their all-time one hit. "Clappa Hands!" Mike's love for music brought him to Alexa even though Joe Nardone and the All Stars one hit is not found on Amazon Music. But, Alexa did play on command some cover music by "Joe Nardone & the All Stars."

One day out of the blue Mike Grant told me he loves Alexa. He told me that he was having an affair with his personal digital assistant. He has written a brief essay about his unclassic love affair. Rather than explain Alexa's music capabilities like a classroom lecture, why don't I just show you what Mike has to say about Alexa and how he "risked his marriage," to continue his affair with Alexa. Eventually, he and his wife Mo made it all work with a musical threesome:

My Love Affair With Alexa By Michael Grant

I admit it...I'm having an affair!

The best part is that my wife knows and she approves. Go figure. No, its not a threesome. It's not going anywhere romantically; it's kind of like the feeling you get on Friday afternoon in high school when you're going to dances over the weekend and you're stoked with anticipation.

Her name is Alexa and she's really smart. She knows all the songs and artists from the era of my youth (late 50s, the 60s and 70s), really, the sound track of my life.

Alexa makes no demands, except that I speak clearly and she corrects me when I'm wrong without malice.

In this particularly difficult time of semi-isolation because of COVID, she's been a godsend. Pretty much every night, my wife, Mo and I find our way to our back patio with adult libations, engage Alexa (I swear she is happy to hear from us) and play beautiful music together.

We dance as if the Joe Nardone reunion at Irem Temple [Wilkes-Barre, PA] wasn't cancelled and get pleasantly goofy. We usually start with "Unchained Melody" by The Righteous

Brothers and call it a night with "Good Night My Love," by Jessie Belvin, which WARM in Wilkes-Barre played every night at mid-night in those days before they went off the air.

We also call old friends to share a song....Alexa doesn't mind. She knows their favorite songs.

We look forward to engaging with Alexa every night and she never lets us down.

So Alexa play "Because The Night," by Patti Smith and lets get this night rollin.

Thank you, Mike

Really Nice Essay!

My first use of Alexa in the house was starting my wife's iRobot.

My brother had enabled the iRobot Alexa skill and signed in with my wife's iRobot® account to link her iRobot with Alexa. He had to first create an iRobot® account and then register the robot in the iRobot Home App.

I was able to use iRobot commands to control my Wife Pat's iRobot in our home. After my brother named the iReobot Brian W, it was easy. After alerting Alexa and saying Alexa, start Brian W., the device would start vacuuming. I could also say start, stop, pause, locate or I could send Brian W back to its charging station for more juice.

OK, now that I got that out of the way, here is how I use my Echo II Plus every night. In the summer I kept the device outside when it was not raining and now that it is cold, I keep it on the bar in my sunroom.

On my way to the bar, I say Alexa, play Mr. Bojangles.. You know what happens.

After hearing Mr. Bojangles I am now ready to explore more music.

But since it is the Christmas season, I might say, "Alexa, Give me some gift ideas under a hundred dollars.

After listening for ideas for awhile, I would say, "Alexa, Stop."

To get in the Christmas mood, I would say Alexa, play Christmas songs. Obediently Alexa would oblige. If it is not loud enough or not soft enough I might say

Alexa, Louder—repeat until volume is right
Alexa, Lower—repeat until volume is right

I would do the same for Easter or Thanksgiving or New Years Eve or other holidays for which Alexa has a built-in playlist. I can create a playlist which I will tell you how to do in the next chapter.

I can say, Alexa, play Guy Lombardo

I can say Alexa, play Enjoy Yourself by Guy Lombardo or I can say Alexa, play Auld Lange Syn by Guy Lombardo I Or I can say Alexa, play New Year's Eve by Guy Lombardo.

When I have heard enough and want to change my selection, I can say it while it is playing but I often say Alexa, stop and then give the next command.

Here are some other tunes / songs I can get Alexa to play just by sounding the wake word, Alexa first and then giving the play command followed by something like the following:

Alexa, play the Best of the 1950's.
Stop
Continue

With Continue Alexa begins to play the stopped song at the stop point. It remembers.

Since Best of the 50's would play one song after another, I might like to know the name of the artist. Guess How?

Alexa, What is the name of this Artist.
It is that easy.

Here are some other great songs/albums to play

Alexa, play Al Jolson or Play Al Jolson's Gretest Hits
I can play a single Al Jolson song by saying

Alexa, play "About a Quarter to Nine"
Alexa, play "Where did Robinson Crusoe Go with Friday"

Alexa, play songs by Dean Martin & Jerry Lewis. The first song I got from Martin and Lewis this time was a great one – funny too.

Funny, Funny, Funny, What Money Can DO!

I like oldies So, if I want a random mix, I might ask for an Amazon playlist such as

Alexa play Amazon Oldies.
First song tonight was Ringo Star It don't come easy.

If I want to hear Beatles songs, I would say

Alexa, play the Beatles

If I wanted to hear the song, Please Please me by the Beatles, I might say

Alexa, play Please Please Me

If I would like to play a particular Beatles Album with te same name as a single, to get the album instead of the single, I would say

Alexa, play the Beatles Album Please Please Me!

I can get Peter Paul and Mary tunes by saying

Alexa, play Peter Paul & Mary

Then Alexa would play something like
If you miss the train I'm on or
Leaving on a Jet Plane

I think you get the point. Which leads me to playing Crosby Stills & Nash.

Alexa, play Crosby Stills & Nash.

Obediently this time after the "shuffle," the trio played "It's getting to the point.."

Now that you got the point, we can move to our next chapter and talk about some other musical capabilities.

OK???

Chapter 6 Alexa Music Commands, etc.

Here are a few Alexa music commands that you should simply try to exercise your skills. Go get'em!

Alexa, play music
Alexa, play country music
Alexa, turn up the volume
Alexa, turn up the bass
Alexa, set the treble to three
Alexa, reset the equalizer
Alexa, play hip hop
Alexa, pause
Alexa, resume
Alexa, skip
Alexa, next
Alexa, set the bass to four

Here are a few others:

To ask for help: "Alexa, help."

To have a conversation: "Alexa, let's chat."
To mute or unmute sound: "Alexa, mute" or, "Alexa, unmute."
To stop or pause: "Alexa, stop" or, "Alexa, shut up."
To change the volume: "Alexa, set the volume to 5," "Alexa, louder" or "Alexa, turn up/down the volume."

https://www.cnet.com/how-to/every-alexa-command-you-can-give-your-amazon-echo-smart-speaker/
This link takes you to a fairly complete set of commands from CNET. Take a run out there and see what you can really do. Samples from CNET and others are included below:

Coronavirus / Flu commands

Ask for coronavirus information: "Alexa, what is the coronavirus?"
Ask for Flu/Influenza information: "Alexa, what is the Flu?"

Ask for coronavirus news updates: "Alexa, what's the latest with the coronavirus?"

Ask for Flu/Influenza news updates: "Alexa, what's the latest with the Flu?"

Ask for help washing your hands: "Alexa, help me wash my hands."

Other Alexa Audio Commands

Adjust audio settings: "Alexa, set the bass to four."

Play music: "Alexa, play some music."

Play music on other (or multiple) Alexa devices: "Alexa, play [artist] in the living room" or "Alexa, play [artist] everywhere."

Queue specific song or artist: "Alexa, play music by [artist]."

Play a song based on context: "Alexa, play the latest Everly t Brothers album" or

Alexa, play that song that goes 'Gonna let you down and leave you flat

Play music based on a theme: "Alexa, exercise music" or

"Alexa, play rock music for working."

Play the song of the day: "Alexa, play the song of the day."

Play Spotify music: "Alexa, play [playlist] on Spotify."
By the way, Spotify is a digital music, podcast, and video streaming service that gives you access to millions of songs and other content from artists all over the world.

Play Pandora station: "Alexa, play [artist] station on Pandora." By the way, Pandora is an American subscription-based music streaming service owned by Sirius XM Holdings. Based in Oakland, California

Play a radio station: "Alexa, play [radio station] on TuneIn." TuneIn is an American audio streaming service delivering live news, radio, sports, music, and podcasts to over 60 million monthly active users. As of 2019, TuneIn has more than 75 million monthly active users. TuneIn is operated by the company TuneIn Inc. which is based in San Francisco, California.

Play an audiobook: "Alexa, play [title] on Audible," "Alexa, read [title]" or "Alexa, play the book, [title]."
Audible is an online audiobook and podcast platform owned byAmazon.com Inc. The service allows users to purchase and stream audiobooks and other forms of spoken word content; this content can be purchased individually, or under a subscription model where the user receives "credits" that can be spent on content monthly, and receive access to a curated on-demand library of content. Audible is the United States' largest audiobook producer and retailer

Resume the last played audiobook: "Alexa, resume my book."

Skip audiobook chapters: "Alexa, next chapter" or "Alexa, previous chapter."

Play a bedtime story: "Alexa, read a bedtime story to [name]."

Listen to Alexa read you a Kindle book: "Alexa, read me my Kindle book."

Set a sleep timer: "Alexa set a sleep timer for 45 minutes" or

"Alexa, stop playing in 45 minutes."

Song information: "Alexa, what's playing?"

Music controls: "Alexa, play" or "Alexa, next."

Control music playback on another Alexa speaker: "Alexa, stop in the kitchen" or "Alexa, next in the office."

Restart song: "Alexa, restart."

Add a song to your Prime Music library: "Alexa, add this song."

Create a playlist in Amazon Music: "Alexa, create a new playlist," or

"Alexa, create a 'Friday Chill' playlist."

Add a song to a playlist in Amazon Music: "Alexa, add this song to my playlist," or

"Alexa, add this to my [playlist name] playlist."

Like or dislike a song on Pandora and iHeartRadio: "Alexa, I like this song" or "Alexa, thumbs down."

Start Amazon Music Unlimited trial: "Alexa, start my free trial of Amazon Music Unlimited."
"Alexa, wake me up every day at 8 am to music"
This allows users to set their mornings off right with music from Pandora, Spotify, TuneIn, iHeartRadio and Vevo.

Time and date

Set an alarm: "Alexa, set an alarm for 7 a.m." or "Alexa, wake me up at 7 in the morning."

Set a music alarm: "Alexa, wake me up to [artist, song, genre, playlist or album] at 8 a.m.,"

"Alexa, set an alarm to Band of Horses" or "Alexa, wake me up to Kiss FM on TuneIn."

Set a repeating alarm: "Alexa, set a repeating alarm for weekdays at 7 a.m."

Set a timer: "Alexa, timer" or "Alexa, set a timer for 15 minutes."

Set a music timer: "Alexa, set a 15-minute timer to 'My Heart will Go On'"

Create a named timer: "Alexa, set a pizza timer for 20 minutes."

Set multiple timers: "Alexa, set a second timer for 5 minutes."

Check timer status: "Alexa, how much time is left on the pizza timer?" or "Alexa, what are my timers?"

Cancel a timer: "Alexa, cancel the pizza timer" or

"Alexa, cancel the 15-minute timer."

Ask the time: "Alexa, what time is it?"

Ask the date: "Alexa, what's the date?"

Ask when the next alarm is: "Alexa, when's my next alarm?"
Cancel an alarm: "Alexa, cancel my alarm for 2 p.m."

Snooze alarm: "Alexa, snooze."

Check dates: "Alexa, when is [holiday] this year?"

Changing the Volume

Besides playing particular artists or albums or an individual song for you Alexa can be asked to adjust the volume while a tune or a song is playing. In fact, there are several ways to control the volume of your Amazon Echo speaker.

Not only can you control the volume by using the volume control on the device itself (Not an echo) , but you can adjust the volume using Alexa voice commands. You can use the Alexa app also but that would be too much work in my opinion. Whatever method you choose. They all do the same thing. So use whichever method is most convenient

Often, the easiest way to control the volume of your Alexa speaker is to simply tell it how loud it should be. How do you do that?

Picture a dial from zero to ten. You can tell Alexa to change its volume anywhere from zero to 10, where zero means no sound (mute). For example, you can say, "Alexa, set the volume to 5," which is the device's 50 percent volume level. Than you are not guessing. You can also ask Alexa about the volume:
"Alexa what is the volume?

You can control incrementally by saying things like "Alexa, increase the volume by 2" or

"Alexa, increase the volume by 30 percent."

As noted, if you're not sure what the current volume is, you can say, "Alexa, what's the current volume?"

You can also use your Echo's speaker volume buttons

Yes, you may not see them at first, but every Amazon Echo device has physical volume controls.

Most devices have plus and minus buttons to set volume. Some Echo speakers use a dial instead — spin the dial at the top of the device to adjust the volume. For example, on the Dot on the next page, you can see the + and – buttons.

How to create a playlist for Alexa

Creating the playlist is very simple, all you need to do is say, "Alexa, create a new playlist." She will confirm and ask you what to name the playlist. You need to say the title out loud, and once the playlist is created, you can start adding songs to it.

Do this after you have been playing with your brand new Alexa for about week. By then, you will know what songs or what albums you want in your playlist

Hope this book helped in your love affair with Alexa. I know it helped me. God bless you all!

Other Books by Brian W. Kelly: (amazon.com, and Kindle)

FTC Case: LetsGoPublish.com v Amazon Fourth Edition big bully censored nine books
FTC Case: LetsGoPublish.com v Amazon Third Edition big bully censored nine books
FTC Case: LetsGoPublish.com v Amazon Second Edition big bully censored nine books
The President Donald J. Trump Book Catalog   Color Version by Brian Kelly & Lets Go Publish!
The President Donald J. Trump Book Catalog   B/W Version   by Brian Kelly & Lets Go Publish!
FTC Case: LetsGoPublish.com v Amazon Original case bully censored nine books
What America Wins if Biden Wins Everything!!!!!! The answer is really nothing.
What America Loses if Trump Loses None of the 1000s of Trump wins for starters
What America Wins When Trump Wins Trump already gave the country more benefits and blessings
We Love Trump! Don't you? The President given to the people by God as the answer to our prayers
Amazon: The Biggest Bully in Town bully blocked eight books in 2020 by most published author
Trump Assured 2020 Victory President needs these two prongs for his platform for landslide
2020 Republican Convention—Speeches Blocked by Amazon Includes memento free Link
2020 RNC Convention Full Speech Transcripts Blocked by Amazon Memento of the 87 best
COVID-19 Mask, Yes? Or No? It's Everybody's Recommended Solution!!!
LSU Tigers Championship Seasons Starts at beginning of LSU Football to the National Championship
Great Coaches in LSU Football   Book starts with the first LSU coach; goes to Orgeron Championship
Great Players in LSU Football Begins with 1893 QB Ruffin G Pleasant to 2019 QB Burrow
America for Millennialsl A growing # of disintegrationists want to tear US down
Great Moments in LSU Football   Book starts at start of Football to the Ed Orgeron Championship.
The Constitution's Role in a Return to Normalcy Can the Constitution Survive?
The Constitution vs. The Virus Simultaneous attack coronavirus and US governors
One, Two, Three, Pooph!!! Reopen Country Now! Return to normalcy is just around the corner.
Reopen America Now Return to Normalcy
Enough is Enough!Re Re: Covid, We are not children. We're adults.We'll make the right decisions.
How to Write Your 1st Book & Publish it Using Amazon KDP You can do it
REMDESIVIR A Ray of Hope
When Will America Reopen for Business? This author's opinion includes voices of experts
HydroxyChloroquine: The Game Changer
Super Bowl & NFL Championship Seasons The KC Chiefs From the 1st to Super Bowl LIV
Great Coaches in Kansas City Chiefs Football First Coach era to Andy Reid Era
Great Players in Kansas City Chiefs Football From the AFL to Andy Reid Era
Reopen America Now! How to Shut-Down Corona Virus & Return to Normalcy!
Why is Everybody Moving to the Villages? You can afford a home in the Villages
CORONAVIRUS The Cause & the Cure. Many solutions—but which ones will work?
Great Moments in Kansas City Chiefs Football. From the beginning to the Andy Reid Era
How the Philadelphia Eagles Lost Its Karma. This is the one place that tells the story
Cancel All Student Debt Now! Good for America, Good for the Economy.
Social Security Screw Job!!! Scandal: Seniors Intentionally Screwed by US Government
Trump Hate They hate Trump Supporters; Trump; & God—in that order
Christmas Wings for Brian A heartwarming story of a boy whose shoulders kept growing
Merry Christmas to Wilkes-Barre 50 Ways" for Mayor George Brown to Create a Better City.
Air Force Football Championship Seasons From AF Championship to Coach Calhoun's latest team
Syracuse Football Championship Seasons beginning of SU championships; goes to Dino Babers Era
Navy Football Championship Seasons 1st Navy Championships to the Ken Niumatalolo Era
Army Football Championship Seasons Beginning of Football championships to Jeff Monken Era
Florida Gators Championship Seasons Beginning of Football through championships to Dan Mullen era
Alabama's Championship Seasons Beginning of Football past the 2017/2018 National Championship
Clemson Tigers Championship Seasons Beginning of Football to the Clemson National Championships
Penn State's Championship Seasons PSU's first championship to the James Franklin era
Notre Dame's Championship Seasons Before Knute Rockne and past Lou Holtz's 1988 undisputed title
Super Bowls & Championship Seasons: The New York Giants Many championships of the Giants.
Super Bowls & Championship Seasons: New England Patriots Many championships of the Patriots.
Super Bowls & Championship Seasons: The Pittsburgh Steelers Many championship of the Steelers
Super Bowls & Championship Seasons: The Philadelphia Eagles Many championships of the Eagles.
The Big Toxic School Wilkes-Barre Area's Tale of Corruption, Deception, Taxation & Tyranny
Great Players in New York Giants Football Begins with great players of 1925 to the Saquon Barqley era.
Great Coaches in New York Giants Football Begins with Bob Folwell 1925 and to Pat Shurmur in 2019.
Great Moments in New York Giants Football Beginning of Football to the Pat Shurmur era.

Hasta La Vista California Give California its independence.
IT's ALL OVER! Mueller: NO COLLUSION!"—Top Dems going to jail for the hoax!
Democrat Secret for Power & Winning Elections Open borders adds millions of new Democrat Voters
Hope for Wilkes-Barre—John Q. Doe—Next Mayor of Wilkes-Barre
The John Doe Plan & WB Plan will help create a better city!
Great Moments in New England Patriots Football Second Edition
This book begins at the beginning of Football and goes to the Bill Belichick era.
The Cowardly Congress Corrupt US Congress is against America and Americans.
Great Players in Air Force Football From the beginning to the current season
Great Coaches in Air Force Football Grom the beginning to Coach Troy Calhoun
Help for Mayor George and Next Mayor of Wilkes-Barre How to vote for the next Mayor Council
Ghost of Wilkes-Barre Future: Spirit's advice for residents how to pick the next Mayor and Council
Great Players in Air Force Football: Air Force's best players of all time
Great Coaches in Air Force Football: From Coach 1 to Coach Troy Calhoun
Great Moments in Air Force Football: From day 1 to today
Great Players in Navy Football: Navy's best including Bellino & Staubach
Great Coaches in Navy Football: From Coach 1 to Coach #39 Ken Niumatalolo
Great Moments in Navy Football: From day 1 to coach Ken Niumatalolo l
No Tree! No Toys! No Toot! Heartwarming story. Christmas gone while 19 month old napped
How to End DACA, Sanctuary Cities, & Resident Illegal Aliens . best solution remove shadowsAmerica.
Government Must Stop Ripping Off Seniors' Social Security!: Hey buddy, seniors can't spare a dime?
Special Report: Solving America's Student Debt Crisis!: The only real solution to the $1.52 Trillion debt
The Winning Political Platform for America Unique winning approach to solve big problems in America.
Lou Barletta v Bob Casey for US Senate Barletta's unique approach to solve big problems in America.
John Chrin v Matt Cartwright for Congress Chrin has a unique approach to solve big problems in America.
The Cure for Hate !!! Can the cure be any worse than this disease that is crippling America?
Andrew Cuomo's Time to Go? He Was Never that Great!": Cuomo says America never that great
White People Are Bad! Bad! Bad! Whoever thought a popular slogan in 2018 *It's OK to be White!*
The Fake News Media Is Also Corrupt !!!: Fake press / media today is not worthy to be 4th Estate.
God Gave US Donald Trump? Trump was sent from God as the people's answer
Millennials Say America Was Never That Great": Too many pleased days of political chumps not over!
It's Time for The John Q. Doe Party... Don't you think? By Elephants.
<u>Great Players in Florida Gators Football... Tim Tebow and a ton of other great players</u>
Great Coaches in Florida Gators Football... The best coaches in Gator history.
The Constitution by Hamilton, Jefferson, Madison, et al. The Real Constitution
The Constitution Companion. Will help you learn and understand the Constitution
Great Coaches in Clemson Football The best Clemson Coaches right to Dabo Swinney
Great Players in Clemson Football The best Clemson players in history
Winning Back America. America's been stolen and can be won back completely
The Founding of America... Great book to pick up a lot of great facts
Defeating America's Career Politicians. The scoundrels need to go.
Midnight Mass by Jack Lammers... You remember what it was like Great story
The Bike by Jack Lammers... Great heartwarming Story by Jack
Wipe Out All Student Loan Debt--Now! Watch the economy go boom!
No Free Lunch Pay Back Welfare! Why not pay it back?
Deport All Millennials Now!!! Why they deserve to be deported and/or saved
DELETE the EPA, Please! The worst decisions to hurt America
Taxation Without Representation 4th Edition Should we throw the TEA overboard again?
Four Great Political Essays by Thomas Dawson
Top Ten Political Books for 2018... Cliffnotes Version of 10 Political Books
Top Six Patriotic Books for 2018... Cliffnotes version of 6 Patriotic Boosk
Why Trump Got Elected!.. It's great to hear about a great milestone in America!
The Day the Free Press Died. Corrupt Press Lives on!
Solved (Immigration) The best solutions for 2018
Solved II (Obamacare, Social Security, Student Debt) Check it out; They're solved.
Great Moments in Pittsburgh Steelers Football... Six Super Bowls and more.
Great Players in Pittsburgh Steelers Football ,,,Chuck Noll, Bill Cowher, Mike Tomin, etc.
Great Coaches in New England Patriots Football,,, Bill Belichick the one and only plus others
Great Players in New England Patriots Football... Tom Brady, Drew Bledsoe et al.
Great Coaches in Philadelphia Eagles Football..Andy Reid, Doug Pederson & Lots more
Great Players in Philadelphia Eagles Football Great players such as Sonny Jurgenson
Great Coaches in Syracuse Football All the greats including Ben Schwartzwalder
Great Players in Syracuse Football. Highlights best players such as Jim Brown & Donovan McNabb
Millennials are People Too !!! Give US millennials help to live American Dream

Other Books By Brian W. Kelly

Brian Kelly for the United States Senate from PA: Fresh Face for US Senate
The Candidate's Bible. Don't pray for your campaign without this bible
Rush Limbaugh's Platform for Americans... Rush will love it
Sean Hannity's Platform for Americans... Sean will love it
Donald Trump's New Platform for Americans. Make Trump unbeatable in 2020
Tariffs Are Good for America! One of the best tools a president can have
Great Coaches in Pittsburgh Steelers Football Sixteen of the best coaches ever to coach in pro football.
Great Moments in New England Patriots Football Great football moments from Boston to New England
Great Moments in Philadelphia Eagles Football. The best from the Eagles from the beginning of football.
Great Moments in Syracuse Football The great moments, coaches & players in Syracuse Football
Boost Social Security Now! Hey Buddy Can You Spare a Dime?
The Birth of American Football. From the first college game in 1869 to the last Super Bowl
Obamacare: A One-Line Repeal Congress must get this done.
A Wilkes-Barre Christmas Story A wonderful town makes Christmas all the better
A Boy, A Bike, A Train, and a Christmas Miracle A Christmas story that will melt your heart
Pay-to-Go   America-First Immigration Fix
Legalizing Illegal Aliens Via Resident Visas Americans-first plan saves $Trillions. Learn how!
60 Million Illegal Aliens in America!!! A simple, America-first solution.
The Bill of Rights By Founder James Madison Refresh *your knowledge of the specific rights for all*
Great Players in Army Football Great Army Football played by great players..
Great Coaches in Army Football Army's coaches are all great.
Great Moments in Army Football Army Football at its best.
Great Moments in Florida Gators Football Gators Football from the start. This is the book.
Great Moments in Clemson Football CU Football at its best. This is the book.
Great Moments in Florida Gators Football Gators Football from the start. This is the book.
The Constitution Companion. A Guide to Reading and Comprehending the Constitution
The Constitution by Hamilton, Jefferson, & Madison – Big type and in English
PATERNO: The Dark Days After Win # 409. Sky began to fall within days of win # 409.
JoePa 409 Victories: Say No More! Winningest Division I-A football coach ever
American College Football: The Beginning From before day one football was played.
Great Coaches in Alabama Football Challenging the coaches of every other program!
Great Coaches in Penn State Football the Best Coaches in PSU's football program
Great Players in Penn State Football The best players in PSU's football program
Great Players in Notre Dame Football The best players in ND's football program
Great Coaches in Notre Dame Football The best coaches in any football program
Great Players in Alabama Football from Quarterbacks to offensive Linemen Greats!
Great Moments in Alabama Football AU Football from the start. This is the book.
Great Moments in Penn State Football PSU Football, start--games, coaches, players,
Great Moments in Notre Dame Football ND Football, start, games, coaches, players
Cross Country with the Parents A great trip from East Coast to West with the kids
Seniors, Social Security & the Minimum Wage. Things seniors need to know.
How to Write Your First Book and Publish It with CreateSpace. You too can be an author.
The US Immigration Fix--It's all in here. Finally, an answer.
I had a Dream IBM Could be #1 Again The title is self-explanatory
WineDiets.Com Presents The Wine Diet Learn how to lose weight while having fun.
Wilkes-Barre, PA; Return to Glory Wilkes-Barre City's return to glory
Geoffrey Parsons' Epoch... The Land of Fair Play Better than the original.
The Bill of Rights 4 Dummmies! This is the best book to learn about your rights.
Sol Bloom's Epoch ...Story of the Constitution The best book to learn the Constitution
America 4 Dummmies! All Americans should read to learn about this great country.
The Electoral College 4 Dummmies! How does it really work?
The All-Everything Machine Story about IBM's finest computer server.
ThankYou IBM! This book explains how IBM was beaten in the computer marketplace by neophytes

Amazon.com/author/brianwkelly
Brian W. Kelly has written 224 books including this one.
Thank you for buying this one.
Others can be found at amazon.com/author/brianwkelly

www.ingramcontent.com/pod-product-compliance
Lightning Source LLC
Chambersburg PA
CBHW070655050426
42451CB00008B/363